THE HOLY PLACES

NULLA SILVA TALEM PROFERT,
FRONDE, FLORE, GERMINE

THE
HOLY PLACES

BY

EVELYN WAUGH

WITH WOOD ENGRAVINGS BY

REYNOLDS STONE

PUBLISHED BY

THE QUEEN ANNE PRESS LONDON

THE BRITISH BOOK CENTRE NEW YORK

1953

TO

ELIZABETH AND FRANK

PAKENHAM

Work Abandoned

MY first visit to Jerusalem was at Christmas-tide, 1935. I came from embattled Abyssinia. The League of Nations had virtually come to an end that summer. But at Bethlehem and at Calvary were the pilgrims of the world, united in an older and more steadfast friendship. It seemed a place of peace.

Those who lived in Palestine knew otherwise. The Arab Revolt was even then being planned. That Christmas in fact was the last to be celebrated at Bethlehem in complete tranquillity. But the pilgrim was not to know that. The Zionists had not then thrown off their disguise; they showed themselves to the ingenuous as decent, rather cranky young people, innocently occupied in the cultivation of grape-fruit. Jerusalem had all the air of a city of Christendom reclaimed. The prayers which, seventeen years before, had risen in thanks for General Allenby's superbly modest entrance, were still fresh in the memory. The first Christian government since the fall of the Crusaders' kingdom was the purest and the most benevolent which the land had known since the age of Constantine. Fine buildings were being completed everywhere, ancient ones were being restored and embellished. Among the deeper emotions of the pilgrimage was also a deep pride in being English.

I was of an age then—thirty-two—when, after I had struck lucky with three or four light novels, it did not seem entirely absurd, at any rate to myself, to look about for a suitable 'life's work'; (one learns later that life itself is work enough). So elated was I by the beauties about me that I there and then began vaguely planning a series of books—semi-historic, semi-poetic fiction, I did not quite know what—about the long, intricate, intimate relations between England and the Holy Places. The list of great and strange Britons who from time to time embodied the association—Helena, Richard Lionheart, Stratford Canning, Gordon—would without doubt grow with research. Helena above all first began a ferment in my imagination which lasted for fifteen years. I completed a novel about her which failed in most cases to communicate my enthusiasm. I then devised a short explanation for the B.B.C., who were giving a dramatic version of my story. It is this that is here reprinted.

The first, flushed, calf love of my theme has never completely cooled, though I now know that I shall not pursue it further. One element certainly is dead for ever—the pride of country. We surrendered our mandate to rule the Holy Land for low motives: cowardice, sloth and parsimony. The vision of Allenby marching on foot where the Kaiser had arrogantly ridden, is overlaid now by the sorry spectacle of a large, well-found force, barely scratched in battle, decamping before a little gang of gunmen. Palestine is no longer a

2

land where an Englishman can walk with pride. But piety, curiosity and my relish for the idiosyncratic splendour of the place, drew me back. The patronage of the editors of *Life* enabled me to make a long visit last year and the second essay in this book is the report on what I saw, originally written for that magazine. It makes clear, I think, why the life's work I planned will never come to fruit.

STINCHCOMBE 1952   E. W.

St Helena Empress

WE are advised to meditate on the lives of the saints, but the precept originated in the ages when meditation was a more precise and arduous activity than we are tempted to think it to-day. Heavy apparatus has been at work in the last hundred years to enervate and stultify the imaginative faculties. First realistic novels and plays, then the cinema, have made the urban mentality increasingly subject to suggestion, so that it now lapses effortlessly into a trance-like escape from its condition. It is said that great popularity in fiction and film is only attained

5

by works into which readers and audience can trans-
pose themselves and so be vicariously endangered,
loved and applauded. This kind of reverie is not meditation, even when its objects are worthy of high devotion. It may do little harm, perhaps even some little
good, to fall day-dreaming and play the parts of Sir
Thomas More, King Lewis IX or Father Damien. There
are evident dangers in identifying ourselves with Saint
Francis or Saint John of the Cross. We can invoke the
help of the saints and study the workings of God in
them, but if we delude ourselves that we are walking
in their shoes, seeing through their eyes and thinking
with their minds, we lose sight of the one certain
course of our salvation. There is only one saint that
Bridget Hogan can actually become, Saint Bridget
Hogan, and that saint she *must* become, here or in the
fires of purgatory, if she is to enter heaven. She cannot
slip through in fancy-dress, made up as Joan of Arc.

For this reason it is well to pay particular attention
to the saints about whom our information is incom-
plete. There are names in the calendar about which we
know nothing at all except those names, and them
sometimes in a form that would puzzle their contem-
poraries. There are others about whom, humanly
speaking, we know almost everything, who have left
us a conspectus of their minds in their own writings,
who were accompanied through life by pious biogra-
phers recording every movement and saying, who
were conspicuous in the history of their times so that

we can see them from all sides as they impressed friends and opponents. And mid-way between these two groups are the saints who are remembered for a single act.

To this class Helena eminently belongs. In extreme old age, as Empress Dowager, she made a journey into one part of her son's immense dominions, to Jerusalem. From that journey spring the relics of the True Cross that are venerated everywhere in Christendom. That is what we know; most else is surmise.

Helena was at a time, literally, the most important woman in the world, yet we know next to nothing about her. Two places claim to be her birthplace: Colchester in England and Drepanum, a seaside resort, now quite vanished, in Turkey. The evidence for neither is so strong that Englishman or Turk need abandon his pretension. She was probably of modest rank, not servile, not illustrious. Constantius married her early in his rise to power and abandoned her later for a royal match. She may have been brought up at one of the post-stables on an Imperial trunk road and have there attracted Constantius's attention on one of his official journeys. Or she may, conceivably, have been what legend makes her, the daughter of a British Chief. She bore one son, Constantine the Great, probably at Nish in Serbia. After her divorce she settled at Trier (Treves) where the Cathedral probably stands on the foundations of her palace. Almost certainly it was there that she became Christian. Lactantius, who was tutor to

7

her grandson Crispus, may have helped instruct her. At the very end of her life she suddenly emerged for her great adventure. She died at Constantinople and her body was thereupon or later moved to Rome. Her tomb never became a great centre of pilgrimage. She herself seems never to have attracted great personal devotion; but she was a popular saint. Numberless churches are dedicated to her; numberless girls baptized with her name; she appears everywhere in painting, sculpture and mosaic. She has fitted, in a homely and substantial way, into the family life of Christendom.

There is little of heroism or genius in any of this. We can assume that she was devout, chaste, munificent; a thoroughly good woman in an age when palaces were mostly occupied by the wicked; but she lived grandly and comfortably whereas most of the saints in every age have accepted poverty as the condition of their calling. We know of no suffering of hers, physical, spiritual or mental, beyond the normal bereavements, disappointments and infirmities which we all expect to bear. Yet she lived in an age when Christians had often to choose between flight, apostasy or brutal punishment. Where, one may ask, lies her sanctity? Where the particular lesson for us who live in such very different circumstances?

For the world of Constantine, as we catch glimpses of it, is utterly remote from ours. There are certain superficial similarities. Poetry was dead and prose dying. Architecture had lapsed into the horny hands of engineers. Sculpture had fallen so low that in all his empire Constantine could not find a mason capable of decorating his triumphal arch and preferred instead to rob the two-hundred-year-old arch of Trajan. An enormous bureaucracy was virtually sovereign, controlling taxation on the sources of wealth, for the pleasure of city mobs and for the defence of frontiers more and more dangerously pressed by barbarians from the East. The civilized world was obliged to find a new capital. All this seems familiar; but for the event of supreme importance, the victory of Christianity, we can find no counterpart in contemporary history. We cannot by any effort of the imagination share the emotions of Lactantius or Macarius. Helena, more than anyone, stands in the heart of that mystery.

She might claim, like that other, less prudent queen: 'In my end is my beginning.' But for her final, triumphant journey she would have no fame. We should think of her, if at all, as we think of Constantine : someone who neatly made the best of both worlds. The strong purpose of her pilgrimage shed a new and happier light on the long years of uneventful retirement, showing us that it was by an act of will, grounded in patience and humility, that she accepted her position. Or rather, her positions. We do not know in exactly what state Constantius found her. She certainly did not choose him for his hopes of power. Those hopes, indeed, proved her undoing and dismissed her, divorced, into exile. In

9

a court full of intrigue and murder she formed no party, took no steps against her rival, but quietly accepted her disgrace. Constantine rose to power, proclaimed her empress, struck coins in her honour, opened the whole imperial treasury for her use. And she accepted that, too. Only in her religious practices did she maintain her private station, slipping in to mass at Rome among the crowd, helping with the housework at the convent on Mount Sion. She accepted the fact that God had His own use for her. Others faced the lions in the circus; others lived in caves in the desert. She was to be St. Helena Empress, not St. Helena Martyr or St. Helena Anchorite. She accepted a state of life full of dangers to the soul in which many foundered, and she remained fixed in her purpose until at last it seemed God had no other need of her except to continue to the end, a kind, old lady. Then came her call to a single peculiar act of service, something unattempted before and unrepeatable—the finding of the True Cross.

We have no absolute certainty that she found it. The old sneer, that there was enough 'wood of the cross' to build a ship, though still repeated, has long been nullified. All the splinters and shavings venerated everywhere have been patiently measured and found to comprise a volume far short of a cross. We know that most of these fragments have a plain pedigree back to the early fourth century. But there is no guarantee which would satisfy an antiquary, of the authenticity of Helena's discovery. If she found the True Cross, it was by direct supernatural aid, not by archaeological reasoning. That, from the first, was its patent of title. There are certain elements about the surviving relics which are so odd that they seem to preclude the possibility of imposture. The 'Label', for example—the inscription *Jesus of Nazareth, King of the Jews*—now preserved in Santa Croce, seems the most unlikely product of a forger's art. And who would have tried to cheat her? Not St. Macarius certainly. But it *is* nevertheless possible that Helena was tricked, or that she and her companions mistook casual baulks of timber, builders' waste long buried, for the wood they sought; that the Label, somehow, got added to her treasure later. Even so her enterprise was something life-bringing.

It is not fantastic to claim that her discovery entitles her to a place in the Doctorate of the Church, for she was not merely adding one more stupendous trophy to the hoard of relics which were everywhere being unearthed and enshrined. She was asserting in sensational form a dogma that was in danger of neglect. Power was shifting. In the academies of the Eastern and South-Eastern Mediterranean sharp, sly minds were everywhere looking for phrases and analogies to reconcile the new, blunt creed for which men had died, with the ancient speculations which had beguiled their minds, and with the occult rites which had for generations spiced their logic.

Another phase of existence which select souls enjoyed when the body was shed; a priesthood; a sacramental system, even in certain details of eating, anointing and washing—all these had already a shadowy place in fashionable thought. Everything about the new religion was capable of interpretation, could be refined and diminished; everything except the unreasonable assertion that God became man and died on the Cross; not a myth or an allegory; true God, truly incarnate, tortured to death at a particular moment in time, at a particular geographical place, as a matter of plain historical fact. This was the stumbling block in Carthage, Alexandria, Ephesus and Athens, and at this all the talents of the time went to work, to reduce, hide and eliminate.

Constantine was no match for them. Schooled on battle-fields and in diplomatic conferences, where retreat was often the highest strategy, where truth was a compromise between irreconcilable opposites; busy with all the affairs of State; unused to the technical terms of philosophy; Constantine, not yet baptized, still fuddled perhaps by dreams of Alexander, not quite sure that he was not himself divine, not himself the incarnation of the Supreme Being of whom Jove and Jehovah were alike imperfect emanations; Constantine was quite out of his depth. The situation of the Church was more perilous, though few saw it, than in the days of persecution. And at that crisis suddenly emerged, God-sent from luxurious retirement in the far

north, a lonely, resolute old woman with a single concrete, practical task clear before her; to turn the eyes
of the world back to the planks of wood on which their
salvation hung.

That was Helena's achievement, and for us who,
whatever our difficulties, are no longer troubled by
those particular philosophic confusions that clouded
the fourth century, it has the refreshing quality that
we cannot hope to imitate it. The Cross is very plain
for us to-day; plainer perhaps than for many centuries.
What we can learn from Helena is something about
the workings of God; that He wants a different thing
from each of us, laborious or easy, conspicuous or
quite private, but something which only we can do and
for which we were each created.

The Defence of
the Holy Places

ON one side a people possessed by implacable resentment, on the other by limitless ambition; between them a haphazard frontier determined by the accidents of battle and still, in spite of the truce, the scene of recurrent acts of atrocity and revenge; on that line and cut through by it, stands the most sacred city in the world.

Publicists and politicians have conspired to forget and to make forgotten this open wound in international honour. On 11th December, 1948, the General Assembly of the United Nations proclaimed Jerusalem unique and granted it international status under United Nations control which neither then nor later was made effective. Now, by a double act of aggression as flagrant as the invasion of South Korea, the city has become a battle-ground temporarily divided between two irreconcilable enemies. One voice only is heard reproaching the nations with their betrayal—the Pope's; but he speaks as always in terms of generations and centuries. When he says that internationalization is the only proper solution of the problem he does not mean that it is expedient to evict the usurpers immediately. The great opportunity has been lost. It will come back one day on the tide of history. Meanwhile the Holy City stands as a chilly monument to the moral confusion of our rulers.

It was typical of this confusion that even at the time when it seemed as though the international politicians were ready to protect Jerusalem, they spoke of it as being 'sacred to three great world religions', suggesting that the rights and claims of Christian, Mohammedan and Jew were similar and equal. In fact there are decisive theological and historical differences. Christianity and Mohammedanism may both reasonably be called 'world religions' in that each offers a cosmic system of the relations of all mankind to God. Judaism is the religion of a particular people, a system of rites and social habits which united and distinguished a nation once dispersed, now partly reassembled in a national state. The Temple of Jerusalem was once the sole focus of Jewish worship. There alone a priestly order sacrificed to the national deity. When the Temple was destroyed by Titus in A.D. 70 the Jewish religion was profoundly changed. Since then there has been no priesthood and no sacrifice. In A.D. 363 the Emperor Julian the Apostate ordered the restoration of the Temple and of its worship, but the work was interrupted by a cataclasm which contemporary witnesses accepted as a divine judgment. Since then no responsible Jew has advocated the rebuilding of the Temple. The meat shortage alone would make the ancient sacrifices impossible. The orthodox Jews, who form some eighteen per cent of the population of Israel, believe that the work can only be undertaken when there is an unmistakable, apocalyptic summons. The ten per cent of dogmatic atheists, of course, expect no such event. The majority of Zionists are being encouraged to see the fulfilment of the Prophecies in the establishment of the State of Israel. For the first time no Jew has access to the Wailing Wall, but it is not in the temper of the new State to lament past glories but instead to exalt present achievements. There is a strong movement to divert the national disposition for mourning into more topical channels. A shrine has been erected under the walls of the old city where the

ashes of Jews murdered by the Germans are unceasingly
venerated. It is probable that this will take the place of
the Wailing Wall in the minds of the next generation.

The Mohammedans were late-comers. Jerusalem
had been the sacred city of Christendom for six hundred years before it fell to Omar. He himself entered
with all reverence and chivalrously refrained from
entering the Holy Sepulchre, an act commemorated in
the neighbouring mosque. It is probable that the
Prophet passed through Jerusalem on his way to
Damascus. It is certain that he picked up a great re-
spect for the place in the garbled versions of Christianity and Judaism which formed the basis of his
meditations. At one time he turned towards Jerusalem
to pray. But in the end he left his bones in Medina and
appointed Mecca as the prime centre of pilgrimage and
devotion. Jerusalem comes third to the Mohammedan
and only one spot there is of supreme importance, the
rock over which the great Dome stands, reputed to be
the altar on which Abraham prepared to sacrifice Isaac;
the foundation of the altar is both the Jewish Holy of
Holies and the taking-off place of the Prophet's
visionary visit to Paradise. It was a Christian church
for three hundred years before Omar and again for a
century under the Crusaders, but it is now recognized
by all as an inalienable Mohammedan possession. It
lies on its great platform on the east of the city with
access through the Golden Gate to the Kingdom of
Jordan. The barrier of its walls makes a clear frontier

between it and the rest of the city and, when internationalization comes, it will be easy to separate it
from the zone and make it an integral part of the Arab
Kingdom.

The rest of the ancient city comprises a dense con-
stellation of Christian Holy Places. This term can be
used loosely to include all properties belonging to
various Christian bodies—convents, hostels, churches
—many of which sprang up in the Holy Land during
the last century of Turkish rule; strictly it should mean
only those places which were venerated before the
Mohammedan invasion as the sites of Christian history. It is to those that the pilgrims flocked, and it was
the chief of these that became the subject of the intricate system of *Status Quo* which was elaborated by
the *firmans* of successive Sultans, recognized by international treaty and by the British during their thirty
years of rule. Of Holy Places in this strict sense there
are some forty in the walled city of Jerusalem and on
the Mount of Olives; seven in the adjoining village of
Bethany and sixteen in and around Bethlehem, which
is five miles distant by the old road, now cut by a Jewish
salient. All these lie in the *de facto* authority of the
Hashamite Kingdom of Jordan. In the State of Israel lie
the Church of the Dormition and the Cenacle under
the walls of the old city, three Holy Places at Ein
Karim, one at Emmaus, nine at Nazareth, five on the
Sea of Galilee, three at Cana, one at Carmel. The most
important of these is Nazareth, which stands in a

peculiar position in Israel. Elsewhere the Jews were able to stampede the inhabitants (who now live in destitution, some half million in the wastes of Jordan alone), and hastily fill their homes with Jewish immigrants. But at Nazareth the Arabs, mostly Christians, remained. They now live under restraint, forbidden to travel outside their area or go to work, as they used, in Haifa. Special police passes are required by foreigners to enter the district. The inhabitants are naturally entirely unsympathetic to the State of Israel and would welcome internationalization.

To move from one part of the Holy Land to the other is almost impossible for a subject of either part. For the foreign pilgrim it is difficult but possible. He must possess duplicate passports, he must be ferried across the line at a prearranged time, normally by the kind offices of his consul; once across there is no return by that route. He must fly out from Amman or drive up to Syria and Lebanon. It may be added that the fictitious rate of exchange makes travel in Israel more costly than anywhere else in the world. That is the trick by which a modern government exacts the dues which were considered intolerably oppressive in the Middle Ages. Indeed the conditions which provoked the First Crusade were scarcely more offensive to the pilgrim than those existing today.

But we should not protest too much. It is in the nature of a pilgrimage to be uncomfortable. Often they are undertaken as penance and early rules for pilgrims enjoin bare feet and uncombed hair as essential features. St. Patrick's Purgatory in Ireland is today the only place in the world which maintains the full discipline of the primitive Church (though even there the brush and comb are permitted), and it is thronged with penitents.

The pilgrim's instinct is deep-set in the human heart. It is indeed an affair of the heart rather than of the head. Reason tells us that Christ is as fully present in one church as in another, but we know by experience that some churches have what we most inadequately call an 'atmosphere' in which we pray easily, while others do not. How much more is this true of the spots marked by great events and by the devotion of the saints. Stern moralists of the Middle Ages were constantly exhorting their flocks to stay at home and warning them that the spiritual dangers of the wanderer might quite undo the benefits. But the tide was not to be stayed. It flowed ceaselessly to Compostella and Canterbury and Rome and Cologne and to countless shrines all over the ancient world. As soon as one place was desecrated by Mohammedan and Reformer, other places sprang up. In the last hundred years Lourdes and Fatima have taken rank with the great centres of medieval devotion. Restlessness and mere curiosity no doubt have a part (the motives of human action are inextricably mixed), but far above these is the empty human imagination seeking an object for its attention. In this most natural quest the

Holy Land has for the Christian a primacy which Rome itself cannot approach.

Nevertheless it is a fact that many visitors are disconcerted by what they see there. Those who come fresh from the towering splendours of Catholic Europe, find architecture which is often ramshackle, often meanly modern. Those who come from the light, spacious, plain conventicles of Protestant worship, find murky caves cluttered with shabby ornament and echoing with exotic liturgies. Those whose imaginations have been filled from childhood by bright biblical illustrations and such hymns as Mrs. Alexander's *There is a green hill far away*, find a confusing topography in which the Way of the Cross runs through an oriental bazaar. A little girl remarked at Calvary: 'I never knew our Lord was crucified indoors;' she was expressing an uneasiness that troubles many minds; that troubled General Gordon so much that he was impelled to seek the tomb elsewhere and to find it in a site — archaeologically preposterous — which has comforted many bewildered Nordics. 'The Garden Tomb' is what their Sunday School teachers led them to expect, rather than the Graeco-Russian kiosk of 1809 which now sadly crowns the site unearthed by St. Macarius in 326.

This confusion of mind was expounded in the English House of Lords when they debated the antiquities of Jerusalem at the end of the mandate. Their Lordships were then comforted by the suggestion that

22

since there was some doubt in some minds about their authenticity, the Holy Places did not greatly matter. Perhaps most Americans and Englishmen who have not studied the matter, have a vague impression that there has been a good deal of conscious imposture. Certainly no one accepts as *de fide* the authenticity of all.

What I suppose is plain to anyone who accepts the truth of the Gospels, is that Galilee and the district in and around Jerusalem are sacred to the incidents of Our Lord's life, death, resurrection and ascension. It is, moreover, certain that the vast majority of the spots venerated today were those identified by a living tradition in the fourth century and have been continuously recognized ever since. Whether this living tradition erred occasionally and precise spots were over-enthusiastically accepted where a rather vague memory survived, we cannot know. Recent excavations—for example those at the Lithostrotos of Pilate's Judgment Hall—have confirmed tradition. We now know that our forefathers were wrong in supposing that the Ecce Homo Arch was the building from which Christ was exposed to the people. We do know, however, that deep below the present Via Dolorosa there does lie the actual path He trod to Calvary. We cannot know whether the Stations are the exact sites of the various incidents. The Holy Places indeed comprise the whole gamut of credibility from the 'Tomb of Adam' —a fantasy, surely; the fruit of ancient prosaic minds seeking a concrete form for the poetic imagery used of

23

the Atonement—to the rock of Calvary which no one but an ill-informed bigot would attempt to discredit. Between these two extremes the other shrines could be arranged in a rough order of probability, but the question is primarily antiquarian rather than religious. Suppose—though there is no particular reason to do so—that the place of John the Baptist's birth were not where we think, but a few yards away, in another street, even, of the same village, the devotion of centuries has made the traditional site a Holy Place in fact.

This last may be taken as typical of the minor shrines and of the surprises that await the pilgrim. He has come to Ein Karim to see the home of the Baptist. He finds a handsome modern church in the Spanish style. He is led down a precipitous staircase into a small cave where he is invited to kiss a marble boss. This, he is told, is the birthplace of St. John. His guide is a bearded Franciscan. If they have a language in common, and even perhaps if they have not, the pilgrim will be told at length the stories of St. Elizabeth and of Zachary. He may be shown some pottery of Herod's time found on the spot and the mosaic remains of two Byzantine chapels. But the Franciscans of the Custody are seldom archaeologists and never aesthetes. Their first characteristic is tenacity. They inherited the flag of the Crusades in 1291. When the knights and barons retreated, the friars remained. They have stayed on for more than six hundred years with absolute singleness of purpose, undisturbed by theological and artistic fashions, holding fast to the Gospel and to the stony places where it was enacted. Their struggle has swayed back and forth. They have often been cheated and brutally dispossessed of their property; they have also from time to time received fine benefactions. They have more than once in all their undertakings seen the full revolution of the cycle, decay, destruction, restoration, and have learned to avoid undue attachment to their own transient structures. Indeed they seem positively to relish the demolition of buildings which anywhere else would be patiently preserved; give them the chance to put up something brand new, strong and convenient, and the Franciscans of the Custody jump to it. They have no sentiment except the highest. No association later than the Apostles interests them. There is only one 'period' for them; the years of Our Lord. It is not for us to look askance. They have had small help from art connoisseurs during their age-long, lonely sentry-duty.

But the cave, too, is not what we might have expected. These sacred grottoes are everywhere; here, at Nazareth, at Bethlehem, on the Mount of Olives, as far away as the old Christian quarter beyond the walls of Cairo. The early painters loved to elaborate them and the poetic imagination may leap delightedly from these places to the catacombs, to St. Anthony's cell and St. Jerome's, and again to Lourdes; but, by prosaic Franciscan lights, it does seem remarkably odd that St. Elizabeth should go down to the cellar for her *ac-*

couchement. The explanation, I think, is that she did nothing of the kind. The houses of this district mostly stand over honeycombs of natural and hewn cisterns and store rooms. These remain when the houses fall or burn. In identifying a site in the fourth century, villagers would say : 'Here, our fathers have told us, John was born.' Nothing is more natural than that a confusion should occur and the cave usurp the history of the former house. We may explain in the same way such objects of veneration as the block of stone from which Our Lord is said to have mounted the ass for his entry into Jerusalem. It is probable that the stone was first put there simply to mark the spot and that later generations made it a participant in the actual drama. Concessions such as these are all that need be made to the sceptic. We may admit, too, that the sites of the Dormition and Our Lady's Tomb have strong rivals at Ephesus. But when all these small debts to plausibility have been paid in full, the residual wealth of the Holy Land in authentic gilt-edged association is incomparably large. The supreme treasury is, of course, the great Church of the Holy Sepulchre in Jerusalem.

And here, as one might expect, one finds exemplified and accentuated all the peculiarities of the Holy Land. The first impression, as one enters the courtyard, is that one has come inopportunely. The steps by which one approaches are arched over with a structure of steel girders and wood props; the fine, twelfth-century facade and entrance are entirely obscured by scaffolding. Inside, as one's eyes become accustomed to the gloom, one finds that all the arches of choir and rotunda are reinforced with a dense armature of timber, that everywhere a forest of beams and struts spreads between the ancient columns, and that the walls are bound like a clumsily wrapped parcel with a tangle of steel ties. There has been some recent mishap or some defect has suddenly become apparent, the visitor supposes. Work must be in progress; the men are just on holiday. But such is not the case. The disturbance took place in 1927. Grave danger to the whole fabric was apparent seven years later and these girders and baulks of timber are the hasty improvisations of local British engineers, a first-aid treatment while the ecclesiastical authorities were deciding on a plan. In 1942 further dangers were discerned and further temporary measures taken by the same engineers. Now they have gone away; nothing is being done. The dead hand of the old Ottoman *firmans* and the Treaty of Berlin of 1878 renders the ecclesiastical authorities powerless. They are merely waiting for the inevitable collapse, perhaps in their time, perhaps in the time of their successors, when the Christian world will be obliged to turn its attention to its principal shrine.

Meanwhile one wanders backward through history. One notices first the work of the English sappers, next the reconstruction of the Greek builders of 1810; then, if one has an eye for architecture, one sees that all these encumbrances stand in a great Transitional-

Norman Cathedral, still almost intact; then one may find tucked away underground all that is left of the original buildings of Constantine and Helena. That great assembly of buildings was destroyed by the Persians before the Mohammedan invasions, by Chosroes in 614, who carried off the True Cross. The Emperor Heraclius was the first true Crusader. Solemnly dedicating his arms, he invaded Persia eight years later and brought the relic home in triumph, while the monk Modestus travelled throughout the Empire raising funds for the rebuilding. The fortunes of the shrine were inextricably interlocked with the history of that land of earthquake, invasion and civil riot. Damage, restoration, damage, succeed one another through the centuries. Certain events are of determining importance. This destruction by Chosroes and rebuilding by Modestus and Heraclius is one of them; next, very soon after, the surrender of the city to the Caliph Omar in 637. His Mohammedan successors did not emulate his chivalry. In 1009 the Caliph Hakim, an Egyptian, tried to extirpate Christianity in his dominions. He was probably insane. He reversed his policy later but not before the Church of Modestus had been demolished and the Sepulchre itself, which until then had preserved its original rock-hewn form, had lost roof and walls so that nothing now remains except the floor and the slab upon which Our Lord's body lay. Succeeding *edicules* have been of masonry. It was not until forty years later that the local Christians, with the help of the Emperor Monomachus, were able to complete a rebuilding which lacked most of the splendour of its predecessors and left half the former shrine in ruins. Hakim's persecution shocked Christendom. It was thought intolerable that the Holy City should be at the mercy of the caprices of Mohammedan potentates.

The Emperor of the East had become a reduced and localized power scarcely able to maintain himself at Constantinople, still less to reconquer Palestine. The crusade was preached in the West. In 1099 a Christian army recaptured Jerusalem and established a Latin Kingdom there which survived for barely a century. Under this rule was built the church which stands to-day, enclosing under a single roof the sites of the Crucifixion and the Resurrection. But meanwhile the Great Schism had occurred. On 16th July, 1054, the bickerings of two hundred years took violent form in the excommunication by the Papal Legates of the Patriarch of Constantinople in his own cathedral. The Patriarchs of Alexandria, Antioch and Jerusalem followed him into schism. This was an event quite different from any of the previous outbreaks of heresy. From time to time in the preceding centuries individuals, representing every aberration of theology, had broken from the Universal Church, taking with them numbers of adherents. Most of these bodies disappeared in a generation unless kept alive by particular racial loyalties. But the separation of four historic orthodox patriarchates, on personal and political grounds chiefly, was a disaster from which Christendom still terribly suffers today. It was recognized as something unnatural and deplorable even when tempers were most exacerbated. There were continual attempts at reconciliation. In 1439 at the Council of Florence peace was made, but by that time the Greek clergy had become crassly sectarian and they repudiated their leaders. Nevertheless when Constantinople fell in 1453 St. Sophia was again a Catholic Church as it had been in its first days. The last Emperor of the East died a Catholic, gallantly fighting on the walls. Congregations all over the Levant remained loyal to Rome and survive prosperously today. But, as the whole of Eastern Christendom fell under the Turk, an iron curtain descended between it and the West behind which the great majority of Orthodox Christians was caught at an unpropitious moment. Their schism became the badge of their loyalty. Untouched by humanism, by the stimulating controversy of the fifteenth century, by the great revitalizing power of the Counter-Reformation, cut off from the sap of Christian fellowship, the Eastern Churches dried up and hardened.

Thus were born the disputes over the Holy Places which in their turn produced the *Status Quo*. As the Turkish power matured and softened, the administration relied more and more upon the clever subject peoples for its courtiers and civil servants. Persecution alternated with appeasement in the policy towards Greeks, Armenians and Copts. The cheapest form of appeasement is always to pay with the property of others, and throughout the eighteenth century, as the mind of Europe grew less religious and the sovereigns fought for colonies in the New World and Russia gradually emerged as a great Orthodox Christian power, the Sultans granted more and more licences to the Eastern clergy for encroachment on the rights of the Latins, until by 1757 an immensely complex code was evolved defining precisely how many lamps each cult might hang and on how many feet of ground they might worship at each holy place. France had been the recognized protector of the Catholics in the East. At the Revolution France became atheist. At the height of the Napoleonic regime a fire took place in the Church of the Sepulchre. While the West was indifferent and preoccupied, the Greeks acted, swept away the tombs of the Latin Kings and the Latin choir and reconstructed all they could in their own characteristic style. That is the Church we see today. The Treaties of Paris of 1855, and of Berlin in 1878, reaffirmed the *Status Quo* of 1757 as far as concerned the other Holy Places.

The principle of the *Status Quo* was that property belonged to whoever could prove that he had last exercised the right of repairing it. While certain places were subdivided, others were left as common property of the Catholics, Greeks and Armenians. Nothing can be done to common property, which includes the general fabric of the Church of the Holy Sepulchre, without the consent and participation of all. There is thus a complete *impasse* in which the place is visibly falling to pieces. It may be noted in passing that when a small fire recently occurred in the dome, King Abdullah patched it up without consulting anyone and without anyone minding. He also broke with Turkish precedent in appointing, on 5th January, 1951, an official of his own as Curator of the Holy Places. No one seems to know what this official's duties are. He offers no explanation. What is certain is that the Kingdom of Jordan has not the means to effect the huge repairs that are urgently needed.

In this situation a totally new plan has been produced under the patronage of the Apostolic Delegate in Jerusalem. It is one of total demolition and rebuilding. Two Italian architects—Barluzzi and Marangoni—have produced a pretty album of their designs—*Il Santo Sepolchro di Gerusalemme: Splendori—Miserie —Speranze*—at the Institute of Art at Bergamo, in which is envisaged a scheme of town clearance, demanding a whole quarter of the densely populated city, demolishing two mosques including the historic site of Omar's Prayer, and the ancient convents that now cluster round the basilica, and planting in the centre of this space a huge brand-new edifice where Calvary and the Sepulchre would stand, as they did under Constantine, as separate buildings in an open court. Centred in this court would stand the churches of all the rites which have claims in the existing building and also of the Anglican Church which has not.

No one, I think, regards this undertaking as practicable; few as desirable. Apart from any aesthetic objection—and there are many—there is the supreme objection that this immense erection would be in effect a monument to the divisions of the Church. These divisions are so much a part of the tradition and daily lives of the Franciscans of the Custody that it is small wonder if they have come to accept them as normal and permanent. But there is all the difference between a quarrelsome family who still share one home and jostle one another on the stairs, and one which has coldly split up into separate, inaccessible households. The extreme animosities of the past have subsided, but it is not impossible that they should break out anew. The clergy of the different rites treat one another with courtesy, but they are constantly vigilant; no quarrels have recently occurred because the *Status Quo* has been rigidly observed. Any infringement of it would provide immediate protest and, perhaps, retaliation. It is, of course, all very unseemly and unedifying. But so also is the division of the Church. Under the proposed reconstruction there would be no fear of friction. It would be a great deal more convenient for everyone concerned. But ease would have been bought by the formal perpetuation of a disgrace.

What is needed, surely, is not the grandiose Franciscan plan, but a patient restoration of the building as it stood in 1800? This, indeed, would be no small task, but no greater than the restoration of Rheims

Cathedral after the First World War and of far wider
significance. If the funds and the direction came from
some source quite unconnected with any of the rival
religious bodies, their consent would doubtless be ob-
tainable. It is a task for which the United Nations are
eminently suited. They owe a heavy debt to the Holy
City. This might form a token payment.

But even in its decrepit and defaced condition the
great church is an inspiration, for the whole history
of Christendom is there to be read by those who
trouble to study it. Even the superstitions of early
science have their monument in the stone called 'the
centre of the earth'. Every degree of pilgrim and tourist
pass and repass all day long, with every degree of piety
and insolence, but at night the place really comes to
life.

There is only one door now. It shuts at sundown.
Just before that hour an Arab soldier clears the darken-
ing aisles of the last penitents and sightseers. The Arab
doorkeeper, whose family have held the office since
the time of Suleiman the Magnificent—since Omar
some will tell you—climbs a ladder and turns the locks
from outside, passes the ladder in through a square
trap which a priest locks from his side. The windows
fade and disappear, the roof is lost. There is no light
except from the oil lamps which glow on Calvary,
before the Sepulchre and over the Stone of Unction.
Absolute silence falls. The air becomes close and chilly,
with the faintest smell of oil and candle wax and in-

34

cense. The place seems quite empty. But, in fact, there are thirty or more sleeping men tucked away out of sight in various dens and galleries, like bats in a sunless cave. Nothing happens for hours. Some of the oil lamps begin to burn out. You can sit on the doorman's divan and think yourself at the bottom of the sea.

And then, a little before eleven o'clock, lights begin to appear and move in unsuspected apertures and galleries. There is a snuffling and shuffling and from their various lairs—the Greek from a balcony above the rock of Calvary, the Franciscan from a tunnel in the wall beyond the Latin Chapel, the Armenian down an iron fire-escape above the spot of the Stabat Mater— three bearded sacristans appear and begin filling and trimming the lamps. Soon after this there is a sound of door-knocking, knuckles, wooden hammers, a little electric bell somewhere; a yawning and muttering and coughing and rustling.

At 11.30 something like a jungle war-drum starts up. That is the Greeks. Then a great irregular banging together of planks. That is the Armenians. Then two vested thurifers appear and proceed by opposite routes round the whole building, censing every altar with a chinking of brass and clouds of aromatic smoke. Then here and there raw little electric bulbs flash on. The monks and friars assemble in their choirs and just before midnight the night offices start, the severe monotone of the Latins contrasting with the exuberant gaiety of the Armenians who are out of sight, up their iron staircase in their own bright vault, but whose music sounds like a distant village festival of folk-dancing and peasant ballads.

The Latin Office is the most brief. The friars file out into their tunnel. The Greeks and Armenians sing on. And then something new, unexpected and quite delicious stirs the drowsy senses—the sweet, unmistakable smell of new baked bread. It is the Easterns cooking the Hosts for their masses. Mass is said daily in the tomb by the three rites. On some days the Copts celebrate at an altar built against the outer wall. On Sunday morning the Syrians, too, have their service. And daily on the roof, in the sad little African hovels to which they were driven by the rich Armenians, the Monophysite Abyssinians perform their own ancient liturgy.

The Greek mass is the first, followed by the Armenian. There is room only for priest and server in the inner chamber of the Sepulchre. Two or three more kneel in the outer room. The remainder of the choir stand outside. While the Armenian mass is going on the Catholics may be heard not far off in their chapel intoning another office. By 3.30 the *edicule* is clear of the Armenians and the Franciscan sacristan busies himself with a portable altar and the mass furniture of the West. At four o'clock the door is opened. A servant of the Juded family brings the key, which for convenience he now hangs in the Greek convent on the north of the courtyard, and hands it to the representative of the Musedi family. A monk opens the trap-door and pushes out the ladder. With a squeak and a clang the locks are turned and the door swings open. The monks and the gate-keepers salaam and the gate-keepers shuffle back to bed.

At 4.30 the Catholic mass is said in the Sepulchre, followed by others through all the early hours of the morning on Calvary, in the Chapel of the Franks, and in the Latin Chapel. And at dawn as one steps out into the courtyard after one's vigil, one is met by the cry of the *muezzin* from the minaret of Omar's Prayer, proclaiming that there is no God but Allah and Mohammed is his Prophet.

One has been in the core of one's religion. It is all there, with all its human faults and its superhuman triumphs, and one fully realizes, perhaps for the first time, that Christianity did not strike its first root at Rome or Canterbury or Geneva or Maynooth, but here in the Levant where everything is inextricably mixed and nothing is assimilated. In the Levant there works an alchemy the very reverse of the American melting-pot. Different races and creeds jostle one another for centuries and their diversity becomes only the more accentuated. Our Lord was born into a fiercely divided civilization and so it has remained. But our hope must always be for unity, and as long as the Church of the Sepulchre remains a single building, however subdivided, it forms a memorial to that essential hope.

37

POPULE MEUS QUID FECI TIBI?
AUT IN QUO CONTRISTAVI TE?
RESPONDE MIHI

This book, *The Holy Places*, by Evelyn Waugh, was designed by Robert Harling and printed at The Queen Anne Press, London, England, with the title-page set in *Perpetua* and the text in 14-point *Pilgrim*

Published by
The Queen Anne Press London
The British Book Centre New York
during December 1953